STATUTORY SUPPLEMENT TO

THE LAW OF BUSINESS TORTS AND UNFAIR COMPETITION

CASES, MATERIALS, AND PROBLEMS

■ ■ ■

Colin P. Marks
Professor of Law
St. Mary's University School of Law

Douglas K. Moll
Beirne, Maynard & Parsons, L.L.P. Professor of Law
University of Houston Law Center

AMERICAN CASEBOOK SERIES®

WEST ACADEMIC PUBLISHING

American Casebook Series is a trademark registered in the U.S. Patent and Trademark Office.

© 2016 LEG, Inc. d/b/a West Academic
    444 Cedar Street, Suite 700
    St. Paul, MN 55101
    1-877-888-1330

West, West Academic Publishing, and West Academic are trademarks of West Publishing Corporation, used under license.

Printed in the United States of America

ISBN: 978-1-63460-513-7

PREFACE

This supplement includes the Restatement provisions, uniform acts, and statutes needed for the use of our casebook, THE LAW OF BUSINESS TORTS AND UNFAIR COMPETITION: CASES, MATERIALS, AND PROBLEMS (2016). If you have any comments or suggestions when using the supplement, please feel free to contact us. If you notice errors or omissions, please bring them to our attention as well. We very much welcome your feedback, and we'll incorporate as much as we can into the next edition.

We are truly grateful to the following organizations for granting permission to use their materials:

RESTATEMENT (SECOND) OF CONTRACTS. Copyright © 1981 by the American Law Institute. All rights reserved. Reprinted with permission.

RESTATEMENT (SECOND) OF TORTS. Copyright © 1977 by the American Law Institute. All rights reserved. Reprinted with permission.

RESTATEMENT (THIRD) OF TORTS (Tentative Drafts). Copyright © 2012, 2014 by the American Law Institute. All rights reserved. Reprinted with permission.

RESTATEMENT (THIRD) OF RESTITUTION AND UNJUST ENRICHMENT. Copyright © 2011 by the American Law Institute. All rights reserved. Reprinted with permission.

RESTATEMENT (THIRD) OF UNFAIR COMPETITION. Copyright © 1995 by the American Law Institute. All rights reserved. Reprinted with permission.

RESTATEMENT (FIRST) OF TORTS. Copyright © 1934 by the American Law Institute. All rights reserved. Reprinted with permission.

RESTATEMENT (SECOND) OF AGENCY. Copyright © 1958 by the American Law Institute. All rights reserved. Reprinted with permission.

RESTATEMENT (THIRD) OF AGENCY. Copyright © 2006 by the American Law Institute. All rights reserved. Reprinted with permission.

UNIFORM TRADE SECRETS ACT. Copyright © 1985 by the National Conference of Commissioners on Uniform State Laws.

COLIN P. MARKS
DOUGLAS K. MOLL

January 20, 2016

TABLE OF CONTENTS

PREFACE iii

I.   Restatement (Second) of Contracts 1

II.   Restatement (Second) of Torts 5

III.   Restatement (Third) of Torts... 139

IV.   Restatement (Third) of Restitution & Unjust Enrichment 211

V.   Restatement (Third) of Unfair Competition 263

VI.   Lanham Act (15 U.S.C. §§ 1051–1052, 1064, 1114–1117, 1119, 1125, 1127)... 363

VII. Federal Trade Commission Act (15 U.S.C. § 45).............................. 393

VIII. Copyright Act of 1976 (17 U.S.C. § 301).. 401

IX.   Uniform Trade Secrets Act 403

X.   Restatement (First) of Torts 417

XI.   Restatement (Second) of Agency 421

XII. Restatement (Third) of Agency 427

XIII. Computer Fraud and Abuse Act (18 U.S.C. § 1030) 431

XIV. Economic Espionage Act of 1996 (18 U.S.C. §§ 1831–1832)............. 439

XV.   Illinois Trade Secrets Act (765 ILCS §§ 1065/1 to 1065/9) 441

XVI. Maine Revised Statutes (10 M.R.S. §§ 1541–1548) 445

XVII. Racketeer Influenced and Corrupt Organizations Act (18 U.S.C. §§ 224, 1341, 1343, 1961–1964, 2319A; 19 U.S.C. § 1981)... 449

XVIII. Sherman Act (15 U.S.C. §§ 1–2)...................................... 467

XIX. 15 U.S.C. § 4 469

XX.   Clayton Act (15 U.S.C. §§ 15, 15a, 18, 26) 471

XXI. Robinson–Patman Act (15 U.S.C. §§ 13, 13a, 13b, 21a) 477

STATUTORY SUPPLEMENT TO

THE LAW OF BUSINESS TORTS AND UNFAIR COMPETITION

CASES, MATERIALS, AND PROBLEMS

I. RESTATEMENT (SECOND) OF CONTRACTS

(Selected Sections)

■ ■ ■

Table of Sections

Chapter 16. Remedies
Topic 2. Enforcement by Award of Damages

Section

353. Loss Due to Emotional Disturbance
355. Punitive Damages

Chapter 16. Remedies
Topic 2. Enforcement by Award of Damages

§ 353   Loss Due to Emotional Disturbance

Recovery for emotional disturbance will be excluded unless the breach also caused bodily harm or the contract or the breach is of such a kind that serious emotional disturbance was a particularly likely result.

Comment:

a.   Emotional disturbance. Damages for emotional disturbance are not ordinarily allowed. Even if they are foreseeable, they are often particularly difficult to establish and to measure. There are, however, two exceptional situations where such damages are recoverable. In the first, the disturbance accompanies a bodily injury. In such cases the action may nearly always be regarded as one in tort, although most jurisdictions do not require the plaintiff to specify the nature of the wrong on which his action is based and award damages without classifying the wrong. See Restatement, Second, Torts §§ 436, 905. In the second exceptional situation, the contract or the breach is of such a kind that serious emotional disturbance was a particularly likely result. Common examples are contracts of carriers and innkeepers with passengers and guests, contracts for the carriage or proper disposition of dead bodies, and contracts for the delivery of messages concerning death. Breach of such a contract is particularly likely to cause serious emotional disturbance. Breach of other types of contracts, resulting for example in sudden impoverishment or bankruptcy, may by chance cause even more severe emotional disturbance, but, if the contract is not one where this was a particularly likely risk, there is no recovery for such disturbance.

Illustrations:

1.   A contracts to construct a house for B. A knows when the contract is made that B is in delicate health and that proper completion of the work is of great importance to him. Because of delays and departures from specifications, B suffers nervousness and emotional distress. In an action by B against A for breach of contract, the element of emotional disturbance will not be included as loss for which damages may be awarded.

2.   A, a hotel keeper, wrongfully ejects B, a guest, in breach of contract. In doing so, A uses foul language and accuses B of immorality, but commits no assault. In an action by B against A for breach of contract, the element of B's emotional disturbance will be included as loss for which damages may be awarded.

3.   A makes a contract with B to conduct the funeral for B's husband and to provide a suitable casket and vault for his burial. Shortly thereafter, B discovers that, because A knowingly failed to provide a vault with a suitable lock, water has entered it and reinterment is necessary. B suffers shock, anguish and illness as a result. In an action by B against A for breach of contract, the element of emotional disturbance will be included as loss for which damages may be awarded.

4.   The facts being as stated in Illustration 19 to § 351, the element of emotional disturbance resulting from the additional operation will be included as loss for which damages may be awarded.

§ 355   Punitive Damages

Punitive damages are not recoverable for a breach of contract unless the conduct constituting the breach is also a tort for which punitive damages are recoverable.

Comment:

a.   Compensation not punishment. The purposes of awarding contract damages is to compensate the injured party. See Introductory Note to this Chapter. For this reason, courts in contract cases do not award damages to punish the party in breach or to serve as an example to others unless the conduct constituting the breach is also a tort for which punitive damages are recoverable. Courts are sometimes urged to award punitive damages when, after a particularly aggravated breach, the injured party has difficulty in proving all of the loss that he has suffered. In such cases the willfulness of the breach may be taken into account in applying the requirement that damages be proved with reasonable certainty (Comment *a* to § 352); but the purpose of awarding damages is still compensation and not punishment, and punitive damages are not appropriate. In exceptional instances, departures have been made from this general policy. A number of states have enacted statutes that vary the rule stated in this Section, notably in situations involving consumer transactions or arising under insurance policies.

Illustrations:

1.   A is employed as a school teacher by B. In breach of contract and without notice B discharges A by excluding him from the school building and by stating in the presence of the pupils that he is discharged. Regardless of B's motive in discharging A, A cannot recover punitive damages from B. A can recover compensatory damages under the rule stated in § 347, including any damages for emotional disturbance that are allowable under the rule stated in § 353.

2.   A and B, who are neighbors, make a contract under which A promises to supply water to B from A's well for ten years in return for B's promise to make monthly payments and share the cost of repairs. After several years, the relationship between A and B deteriorates and A, in breach of contract and to spite B, shuts off the water periodically. B cannot recover punitive damages from A. B can recover compensation damages under the rule stated in § 347 if he can prove them with reasonable certainty (§ 352), and the court may take into account the willfulness of A's breach in applying that requirement. See Comment *a* to § 352.

   b.   Exception for tort. In some instances the breach of contract is also a tort, as may be the case for a breach of duty by a public utility. Under modern rules of procedure, the complaint may not show whether the plaintiff intends his case to be regarded as one in contract or one in tort. The rule stated in this Section does not preclude an award of punitive damages in such a case if such an award would be proper under the law of torts. See Restatement, Second, Torts § 908. The term "tort" in the rule stated in this Section is elastic, and the effect of the general expansion of tort liability to protect additional interests is to make punitive damages somewhat more widely available for breach of contract as well. Some courts have gone rather far in this direction.

Illustrations:

3.   A, a telephone company, contracts with B to render uninterrupted service. A, tortiously as well as in breach of contract, fails to maintain service at night and B is unable to telephone a doctor for his sick child. B's right to recover punitive damages is governed by Restatement, Second, Torts § 908.

4.   A borrows money from B, pledging jewelry as security for the loan. B, tortiously as well as in breach of contract, sells the jewelry to a good faith purchaser for value. A's right to recover punitive damages is governed by Restatement, Second, Torts § 908.